'. . . ever-present, phantom thing; My slave, my comrade, and my king'

EMILY BRONTË

Born 1818, Thornton, England
Died 1848, Haworth, England

Poems in this book taken from Janet Gezari's edition of
The Complete Poems, first published by Penguin Books in 1992.
The poem 'Often rebuked, yet always back returning' is
now widely felt to be by Charlotte Brontë, but is too
wonderful to be excluded.

BRONTË IN PENGUIN CLASSICS
The Complete Poems
Wuthering Heights

EMILY BRONTË

The Night is Darkening Round Me

PENGUIN BOOKS

PENGUIN CLASSICS

Published by the Penguin Group
Penguin Books Ltd, 80 Strand, London WC2R ORL, England
Penguin Group (USA) Inc., 375 Hudson Street, New York, New York 10014, USA
Penguin Group (Canada), 90 Eglinton Avenue East, Suite 700, Toronto, Ontario,
Canada M4P 2Y3 (a division of Pearson Penguin Canada Inc.)
Penguin Ireland, 25 St Stephen's Green, Dublin 2, Ireland
(a division of Penguin Books Ltd)
Penguin Group (Australia), 707 Collins Street, Melbourne, Victoria 3008, Australia
(a division of Pearson Australia Group Pty Ltd)
Penguin Books India Pvt Ltd, 11 Community Centre, Panchsheel Park,
New Delhi – 110 017, India
Penguin Group (NZ), 67 Apollo Drive, Rosedale, Auckland 0632, New Zealand
(a division of Pearson New Zealand Ltd)
Penguin Books (South Africa) (Pty) Ltd, Block D, Rosebank Office Park,
181 Jan Smuts Avenue, Parktown North, Gauteng 2193, South Africa

Penguin Books Ltd, Registered Offices: 80 Strand, London WC2R ORL, England

www.penguin.com

This selection published in Penguin Classics 2015
001

Set in 9/12.4 pt Baskerville 10 Pro
Typeset by Jouve (UK), Milton Keynes
Printed in Great Britain by Clays Ltd, St Ives plc

A CIP catalogue record for this book is available from the British Library

ISBN: 978–0–141–39847–1

www.greenpenguin.co.uk

Contents

1. Faith and Despondency

'The winter wind is loud and wild,
Come close to me, my darling child;
Forsake thy books, and mateless play;
And, while the night is gathering grey,
We'll talk its pensive hours away; –

     'Iernë, round our sheltered hall
November's gusts unheeded call;
Not one faint breath can enter here
Enough to wave my daughter's hair,
And I am glad to watch the blaze
Glance from her eyes, with mimic rays;
To feel her cheek so softly pressed,
In happy quiet on my breast.

     'But, yet, even this tranquillity
Brings bitter, restless thoughts to me;
And, in the red fire's cheerful glow,
I think of deep glens, blocked with snow;
I dream of moor, and misty hill,
Where evening closes dark and chill;
For, lone, among the mountains cold,
Lie those that I have loved of old.
And my heart aches, in hopeless pain
Exhausted with repinings vain,
That I shall greet them ne'er again!'

'Father, in early infancy,
When you were far beyond the sea,
Such thoughts were tyrants over me!
I often sat, for hours together,
Through the long nights of angry weather,
Raised on my pillow, to descry
The dim moon struggling in the sky;
Or, with strained ear, to catch the shock,
Of rock with wave, and wave with rock;
So would I fearful vigil keep,
And, all for listening, never sleep.
But this world's life has much to dread,
Not so, my Father, with the dead.

'Oh! not for them, should we despair,
The grave is drear, but they are not there;
Their dust is mingled with the sod,
Their happy souls are gone to God!
You told me this, and yet you sigh,
And murmur that your friends must die.
Ah! my dear father, tell me why?
For, if your former words were true,
How useless would such sorrow be;
As wise, to mourn the seed which grew
Unnoticed on its parent tree,
Because it fell in fertile earth,
And sprang up to a glorious birth –
Struck deep its root, and lifted high
Its green boughs, in the breezy sky.

'But, I'll not fear, I will not weep
For those whose bodies rest in sleep, –
I know there is a blessed shore,
    Opening its ports for me, and mine;
And, gazing Time's wide waters o'er,
    I weary for that land divine,
Where we were born, where you and I
Shall meet our Dearest, when we die;
From suffering and corruption free,
Restored into the Deity.'

'Well hast thou spoken, sweet, trustful child!
    And wiser than thy sire;
And worldly tempests, raging wild,
    Shall strengthen thy desire –
Thy fervent hope, through storm and foam,
    Through wind and ocean's roar,
To reach, at last, the eternal home,
    The steadfast, changeless, shore!'

2. Stars

Ah! why, because the dazzling sun
    Restored our Earth to joy,
Have you departed, every one,
    And left a desert sky?

All through the night, your glorious eyes
    Were gazing down in mine,
And with a full heart's thankful sighs,
    I blessed that watch divine.

I was at peace, and drank your beams
    As they were life to me;
And revelled in my changeful dreams,
    Like petrel on the sea.

Thought followed thought, star followed star,
    Through boundless regions, on;
While one sweet influence, near and far,
    Thrilled through, and proved us one!

Why did the morning dawn to break
    So great, so pure, a spell;
And scorch with fire, the tranquil cheek,
    Where your cool radiance fell?

Blood-red, he rose, and, arrow-straight,
    His fierce beams struck my brow;
The soul of nature, sprang, elate,
    But *mine* sank sad and low!

My lids closed down, yet through their veil,
    I saw him, blazing, still,
And steep in gold the misty dale,
    And flash upon the hill.

I turned me to the pillow, then,
    To call back night, and see
Your worlds of solemn light, again,
    Throb with my heart, and me!

It would not do – the pillow glowed,
    And glowed both roof and floor;
And birds sang loudly in the wood,
    And fresh winds shook the door;

The curtains waved, the wakened flies
    Were murmuring round my room,
Imprisoned there, till I should rise,
    And give them leave to roam.

Oh, stars, and dreams, and gentle night;
    Oh, night and stars return!
And hide me from the hostile light,
    That does not warm, but burn;

That drains the blood of suffering men;
    Drinks tears, instead of dew;
Let me sleep through his blinding reign,
    And only wake with you!

3. The Philosopher

'Enough of thought, philosopher!
    Too long hast thou been dreaming
Unenlightened, in this chamber drear,
    While summer's sun is beaming!
Space-sweeping soul, what sad refrain
Concludes thy musings once again?

    ' "Oh, for the time when I shall sleep
        Without identity,
    And never care how rain may steep,
        Or snow may cover me!
    No promised heaven, these wild desires,
        Could all, or half fulfil;
    No threatened hell, with quenchless fires,
        Subdue this quenchless will!" '

'So said I, and still say the same;
    Still, to my death, will say –
Three gods, within this little frame,
    Are warring night and day;
Heaven could not hold them all, and yet
    They all are held in me;
And must be mine till I forget
    My present entity!
Oh, for the time, when in my breast
    Their struggles will be o'er!
Oh, for the day, when I shall rest,
    And never suffer more!'

'I saw a spirit, standing, man,
    Where thou doth stand – an hour ago,
And round his feet three rivers ran,
    Of equal depth, and equal flow –
A golden stream – and one like blood;
    And one like sapphire seemed to be;
But, where they joined their triple flood
    It tumbled in an inky sea.

The spirit sent his dazzling gaze
    Down through that ocean's gloomy night
Then, kindling all, with sudden blaze,
    The glad deep sparkled wide and bright –
White as the sun, far, far more fair
    Than its divided sources were!'

'And even for that spirit, seer,
    I've watched and sought my life-time long;
Sought him in heaven, hell, earth, and air –
    An endless search, and always wrong!
Had I but seen his glorious eye
    Once light the clouds that wilder me,
I ne'er had raised this coward cry
    To cease to think, and cease to be;
I ne'er had called oblivion blest,
    Nor, stretching eager hands to death,
Implored to change for senseless rest
    This sentient soul, this living breath –
Oh, let me die – that power and will
    Their cruel strife may close;
And conquered good, and conquering ill
    Be lost in one repose!'

4. Remembrance

Cold in the earth – and the deep snow piled above thee,
Far, far, removed, cold in the dreary grave!
Have I forgot, my only Love, to love thee,
Severed at last by Time's all-severing wave?

Now, when alone, do my thoughts no longer hover
Over the mountains, on that northern shore,
Resting their wings where heath and fern-leaves cover
Thy noble heart for ever, ever more?

Cold in the earth – and fifteen wild Decembers,
From those brown hills, have melted into spring:
Faithful, indeed, is the spirit that remembers
After such years of change and suffering!

Sweet Love of youth, forgive, if I forget thee,
While the world's tide is bearing me along;
Other desires and other hopes beset me,
Hopes which obscure, but cannot do thee wrong!

No later light has lightened up my heaven,
No second morn has ever shone for me;
All my life's bliss from thy dear life was given,
All my life's bliss is in the grave with thee.

But, when the days of golden dreams had perished,
And even Despair was powerless to destroy;
Then did I learn how existence could be cherished,
Strengthened, and fed without the aid of joy.

Then did I check the tears of useless passion –
Weaned my young soul from yearning after thine;
Sternly denied its burning wish to hasten
Down to that tomb already more than mine.

And, even yet, I dare not let it languish,
Dare not indulge in memory's rapturous pain;
Once drinking deep of that divinest anguish,
How could I seek the empty world again?

5. A Death-Scene

'O Day! he cannot die
When thou so fair art shining!
O Sun, in such a glorious sky,
So tranquilly declining;

'He cannot leave thee now,
While fresh west winds are blowing,
And all around his youthful brow
Thy cheerful light is glowing!

'Edward, awake, awake –
The golden evening gleams
Warm and bright on Arden's lake –
Arouse thee from thy dreams!

'Beside thee, on my knee,
My dearest friend! I pray
That thou, to cross the eternal sea,
Wouldst yet one hour delay:

'I hear its billows roar –
I see them foaming high;
But no glimpse of a further shore
Has blest my straining eye.

'Believe not what they urge
Of Eden isles beyond;
Turn back, from that tempestuous surge,
To thy own native land.

'It is not death, but pain
That struggles in thy breast –
Nay, rally, Edward, rouse again;
I cannot let thee rest!'

One long look, that sore reproved me
For the woe I could not bear –
One mute look of suffering moved me
To repent my useless prayer:

And, with sudden check, the heaving
Of distraction passed away;
Not a sign of further grieving
Stirred my soul that awful day.

Paled, at length, the sweet sun setting;
Sunk to peace the twilight breeze:
Summer dews fell softly, wetting
Glen, and glade, and silent trees.

Then his eyes began to weary,
Weighed beneath a mortal sleep;
And their orbs grew strangely dreary,
Clouded, even as they would weep.

But they wept not, but they changed not,
Never moved, and never closed;
Troubled still, and still they ranged not –
Wandered not, nor yet reposed!

So I knew that he was dying –
Stooped, and raised his languid head;
Felt no breath, and heard no sighing,
So I knew that he was dead.

6. Song

The linnet in the rocky dells,
    The moor-lark in the air,
The bee among the heather bells,
    That hide my lady fair:

The wild deer browse above her breast;
    The wild birds raise their brood;
And they, her smiles of love caressed,
    Have left her solitude!

I ween, that when the grave's dark wall
    Did first her form retain;
They thought their hearts could ne'er recall
    The light of joy again.

They thought the tide of grief would flow
    Unchecked through future years;
But where is all their anguish now,
    And where are all their tears?

Well, let them fight for honour's breath,
    Or pleasure's shade pursue –
The dweller in the land of death
    Is changed and careless too.

And, if their eyes should watch and weep
    Till sorrow's source were dry,
She would not, in her tranquil sleep,
    Return a single sigh!

Blow, west-wind, by the lonely mound,
    And murmur, summer-streams –
There is no need of other sound
    To soothe my lady's dreams.

7. Anticipation

How beautiful the earth is still,
To thee – how full of happiness!
How little fraught with real ill,
Or unreal phantoms of distress!
How spring can bring thee glory, yet,
And summer win thee to forget
December's sullen time!
Why dost thou hold the treasure fast,
Of youth's delight, when youth is past,
    And thou art near thy prime?

When those who were thy own compeers,
Equals in fortune and in years,
Have seen their morning melt in tears,
    To clouded, smileless day;
Blest, had they died untried and young,
Before their hearts went wandering wrong,
Poor slaves, subdued by passions strong,
    A weak and helpless prey!

'Because, I hoped while they enjoyed,
And, by fulfilment, hope destroyed;
As children hope, with trustful breast,
I waited bliss – and cherished rest.
A thoughtful spirit taught me, soon,
That we must long till life be done;
  That every phase of earthly joy
  Must always fade, and always cloy:

'This I foresaw – and would not chase
　　The fleeting treacheries;
But, with firm foot and tranquil face,
Held backward from that tempting race,
Gazed o'er the sands the waves efface,
　　To the enduring seas –
There cast my anchor of desire
Deep in unknown eternity;
Nor ever let my spirit tire,
With looking for *what is to be!*

'It is hope's spell that glorifies,
Like youth, to my maturer eyes,
All Nature's million mysteries,
　　The fearful and the fair –
Hope soothes me in the griefs I know;
She lulls my pain for others' woe,
And makes me strong to undergo
　　What I am born to bear.

'Glad comforter! will I not brave,
Unawed, the darkness of the grave?
Nay, smile to hear Death's billows rave –
　　Sustained, my guide, by thee?
The more unjust seems present fate,
The more my spirit swells elate,
Strong, in thy strength, to anticipate
　　Rewarding destiny!'

8. The Prisoner (A Fragment)

In the dungeon-crypts, idly did I stray,
Reckless of the lives wasting there away;
'Draw the ponderous bars! open, Warder stern!'
He dared not say me nay – the hinges harshly turn.

'Our guests are darkly lodged,' I whisper'd, gazing
    through
The vault, whose grated eye showed heaven more grey
    than blue;
(This was when glad spring laughed in awaking pride;)
'Aye, darkly lodged enough!' returned my sullen guide.

Then, God forgive my youth; forgive my careless tongue;
I scoffed, as chill chains on the damp flag-stones rung:
'Confined in triple walls, art thou so much to fear,
That we must bind thee down and clench thy fetters here?'

The captive raised her face, it was as soft and mild
As sculptured marble saint, or slumbering unwean'd child;
It was so soft and mild, it was so sweet and fair,
Pain could not trace a line, nor grief a shadow there!

The captive raised her hand and pressed it to her brow;
'I have been struck,' she said, 'and I am suffering now;
Yet these are little worth, your bolts and irons strong,
And, were they forged in steel, they could not hold me
    long.'

Hoarse laughed the jailer grim: 'Shall I be won to hear;
Dost think, fond, dreaming wretch, that *I* shall grant thy
     prayer?
Or, better still, wilt melt my master's heart with groans?
Ah! sooner might the sun thaw down these granite stones.

'My master's voice is low, his aspect bland and kind,
But hard as hardest flint, the soul that lurks behind;
And I am rough and rude, yet not more rough to see
Than is the hidden ghost that has its home in me.'

About her lips there played a smile of almost scorn,
'My friend,' she gently said, 'you have not heard me
     mourn;
When you my kindred's lives, *my* lost life, can restore,
Then may I weep and sue, – but never, friend, before!

'Still, let my tyrants know, I am not doomed to wear
Year after year in gloom, and desolate despair;
A messenger of Hope, comes every night to me,
And offers for short life, eternal liberty.

'He comes with western winds, with evening's wandering
     airs,
With that clear dusk of heaven that brings the thickest
     stars.
Winds take a pensive tone, and stars a tender fire,
And visions rise, and change, that kill me with desire.

'Desire for nothing known in my maturer years,
When Joy grew mad with awe, at counting future tears.
When, if my spirit's sky was full of flashes warm,
I knew not whence they came, from sun, or thunder storm.

'But, first, a hush of peace – a soundless calm descends;
The struggle of distress, and fierce impatience ends.
Mute music soothes my breast, unuttered harmony,
That I could never dream, till Earth was lost to me.

'Then dawns the Invisible; the Unseen its truth reveals;
My outward sense is gone, my inward essence feels:
Its wings are almost free – its home, its harbour found,
Measuring the gulf, it stoops, and dares the final bound.

'Oh, dreadful is the check – intense the agony –
When the ear begins to hear, and the eye begins to see;
When the pulse begins to throb, the brain to think again,
The soul to feel the flesh, and the flesh to feel the chain.

'Yet I would lose no sting, would wish no torture less,
The more that anguish racks, the earlier it will bless;
And robed in fires of hell, or bright with heavenly shine,
If it but herald death, the vision is divine!'

She ceased to speak, and we, unanswering, turned to go –
We had no further power to work the captive woe:
Her cheek, her gleaming eye, declared that man had given
A sentence, unapproved, and overruled by Heaven.

9. Hope

Hope was but a timid friend;
    She sat without the grated den,
Watching how my fate would tend,
    Even as selfish-hearted men.

She was cruel in her fear;
    Through the bars, one dreary day,
I looked out to scc hcr thcrc,
    And she turned her face away!

Like a false guard, false watch keeping,
    Still in strife, she whispered peace;
She would sing while I was weeping;
    If I listened, she would cease.

False she was, and unrelenting;
    When my last joys strewed the ground,
Even Sorrow saw, repenting,
    Those sad relics scattered round;

Hope, whose whisper would have given
    Balm to all my frenzied pain,
Stretched her wings, and soared to heaven,
    Went, and ne'er returned again!

10. A Day Dream

On a sunny brae, alone I lay
    One summer afternoon;
It was the marriage-time of May
    With her young lover, June.

From her mother's heart, seemed loath to part
    That queen of bridal charms,
But her father smiled on the fairest child
    He ever held in his arms.

The trees did wave their plumy crests,
    The glad birds carolled clear;
And I, of all the wedding guests,
    Was only sullen there!

There was not one, but wished to shun
    My aspect void of cheer;
The very grey rocks, looking on,
    Asked, 'What do you here?'

And I could utter no reply;
    In sooth, I did not know
Why I had brought a clouded eye
    To greet the general glow.

So, resting on a heathy bank,
    I took my heart to me;
And we together sadly sank
    Into a reverie.

We thought, 'When winter comes again,
    Where will these bright things be?
All vanished, like a vision vain,
    An unreal mockery!

'The birds that now so blithely sing,
    Through deserts, frozen dry,
Poor spectres of the perished spring,
    In famished troops, will fly.

'And why should we be glad at all?
    The leaf is hardly green,
Before a token of its fall
    Is on the surface seen!'

Now, whether it were really so,
    I never could be sure;
But as in fit of peevish woe,
    I stretched me on the moor,

A thousand thousand gleaming fires
    Seemed kindling in the air;
A thousand thousand silvery lyres
    Resounded far and near:

Methought, the very breath I breathed
    Was full of sparks divine,
And all my heather-couch was wreathed
    By that celestial shine!

And, while the wide earth echoing rung
    To their strange minstrelsy,
The little glittering spirits sung,
    Or seemed to sing, to me.

'O mortal! mortal! let them die;
    Let time and tears destroy,
That we may overflow the sky
    With universal joy!

'Let grief distract the sufferer's breast,
    And night obscure his way;
They hasten him to endless rest,
    And everlasting day.

'To thee the world is like a tomb,
    A desert's naked shore;
To us, in unimagined bloom,
    It brightens more and more!

'And could we lift the veil, and give
    One brief glimpse to thine eye,
Thou wouldst rejoice for those that live,
    Because they live to die.'

The music ceased; the noonday dream,
    Like dream of night, withdrew;
But Fancy, still, will sometimes deem
    Her fond creation true.

11. *To Imagination*

When weary with the long day's care,
    And earthly change from pain to pain,
And lost and ready to despair,
    Thy kind voice calls me back again:
Oh, my true friend! I am not lone,
While thou canst speak with such a tone!

So hopeless is the world without;
    The world within I doubly prize;
Thy world, where guile, and hate, and doubt,
    And cold suspicion never rise;
Where thou, and I, and Liberty,
Have undisputed sovereignty.

What matters it, that, all around,
    Danger, and guilt, and darkness lie,
If but within our bosom's bound
    We hold a bright, untroubled sky,
Warm with ten thousand mingled rays
Of suns that know no winter days?

Reason, indeed, may oft complain
    For Nature's sad reality,
And tell the suffering heart how vain
    Its cherished dreams must always be;
And Truth may rudely trample down
The flowers of Fancy, newly-blown:

But, thou art ever there, to bring
    The hovering vision back, and breathe
New glories o'er the blighted spring,
    And call a lovelier Life from Death,
And whisper, with a voice divine,
Of real worlds, as bright as thine.

I trust not to thy phantom bliss,
    Yet, still, in evening's quiet hour,
With never-failing thankfulness,
    I welcome thee, Benignant Power;
Sure solacer of human cares,
And sweeter hope, when hope despairs!

12. *How Clear She Shines*

How clear she shines! How quietly
    I lie beneath her guardian light;
While heaven and earth are whispering me,
    'Tomorrow, wake, but, dream tonight.'
Yes, Fancy, come, my Fairy love!
    These throbbing temples softly kiss;
And bend my lonely couch above
    And bring me rest, and bring me bliss.

The world is going; dark world, adieu!
    Grim world, conceal thee till the day;
The heart, thou canst not all subdue,
    Must still resist, if thou delay!

Thy love I will not, will not share;
    Thy hatred only wakes a smile;
Thy griefs may wound – thy wrongs may tear,
    But, oh, thy lies shall ne'er beguile!
While gazing on the stars that glow
    Above me, in that stormless sea,
I long to hope that all the woe
    Creation knows, is held in thee!

And this shall be my dream tonight;
    I'll think the heaven of glorious spheres
Is rolling on its course of light
    In endless bliss, through endless years;

I'll think, there's not one world above,
    Far as these straining eyes can see,
Where wisdom ever laughed at Love,
    Or Virtue crouched to Infamy;

Where, writhing 'neath the strokes of Fate,
    The mangled wretch was forced to smile;
To match his patience 'gainst her hate,
    His heart rebellious all the while.
Where Pleasure still will lead to wrong,
    And helpless Reason warn in vain;
And Truth is weak, and Treachery strong;
    And Joy the surest path to Pain;
And Peace, the lethargy of Grief;
    And Hope, a phantom of the soul;
And Life, a labour, void and brief;
    And Death, the despot of the whole!

13. Sympathy

There should be no despair for you
    While nightly stars are burning;
While evening pours its silent dew
    And sunshine gilds the morning.
There should be no despair – though tears
    May flow down like a river:
Are not the best beloved of years
    Around your heart for ever?

They weep, you weep, it must be so;
    Winds sigh as you are sighing,
And Winter sheds his grief in snow
    Where Autumn's leaves are lying:
Yet, these revive, and from their fate
    Your fate cannot be parted:
Then, journey on, if not elate,
    Still, *never* broken-hearted!

14. Plead for Me

Oh, thy bright eyes must answer now,
When Reason, with a scornful brow,
Is mocking at my overthrow!
Oh, thy sweet tongue must plead for me
And tell, why I have chosen thee!

Stern Reason is to judgment come,
Arrayed in all her forms of gloom:
Wilt thou, my advocate, be dumb?
No, radiant angel, speak and say,
Why I did cast the world away.

Why I have persevered to shun
The common paths that others run,
And on a strange road journeyed on,
Heedless, alike, of wealth and power –
Of glory's wreath and pleasure's flower.

These, once, indeed, seemed Beings Divine;
And they, perchance, heard vows of mine,
And saw my offerings on their shrine;
But, careless gifts are seldom prized,
And *mine* were worthily despised.

So, with a ready heart I swore
To seek their altar-stone no more;
And gave my spirit to adore
Thee, ever-present, phantom thing;
My slave, my comrade, and my king,

A slave, because I rule thee still;
Incline thee to my changeful will,
And make thy influence good or ill:
A comrade, for by day and night
Thou art my intimate delight, –

My darling pain that wounds and sears
And wrings a blessing out from tears
By deadening me to earthly cares;
And yet, a king, though Prudence well
Have taught thy subject to rebel.

And am I wrong to worship, where
Faith cannot doubt, nor hope despair,
Since my own soul can grant my prayer?
Speak, God of visions, plead for me,
And tell why I have chosen thee!

15. Self-Interrogation

'The evening passes fast away,
    'Tis almost time to rest;
What thoughts has left the vanished day,
    What feelings, in thy breast?'

'The vanished day? It leaves a sense
    Of labour hardly done;
Of little, gained with vast expense, –
    A sense of grief alone!

'Time stands before the door of Death,
    Upbraiding bitterly;
And Conscience, with exhaustless breath,
    Pours black reproach on me:

'And though I've said that Conscience lies,
    And Time should Fate condemn;
Still, sad Repentance clouds my eyes,
    And makes me yield to them!'

'Then art thou glad to seek repose?
    Art glad to leave the sea,
And anchor all thy weary woes
    In calm Eternity?

'Nothing regrets to see thee go –
    Not one voice sobs "farewell",
And where thy heart has suffered so,
    Canst thou desire to dwell?'

'Alas! The countless links are strong
    That bind us to our clay;
The loving spirit lingers long,
    And would not pass away!

'And rest is sweet, when laurelled fame
    Will crown the soldier's crest;
But, a brave heart, with a tarnished name,
    Would rather fight than rest.'

'Well, thou hast fought for many a year,
    Hast fought thy whole life through,
Hast humbled Falsehood, trampled Fear;
    What is there left to do?'

''Tis true, this arm has hotly striven,
    Has dared what few would dare;
Much have I done, and freely given,
    But little learnt to bear!'

'Look on the grave, where thou must sleep,
    Thy last, and strongest foe;
It is endurance not to weep,
    If that repose seem woe.

'The long war closing in defeat,
    Defeat serenely borne,
Thy midnight rest may still be sweet,
    And break in glorious morn!'

16. Death

Death! that struck when I was most confiding
In my certain faith of joy to be –
Strike again, Time's withered branch dividing
From the fresh root of Eternity!

Leaves, upon Time's branch, were growing brightly,
Full of sap, and full of silver dew;
Birds beneath its shelter gathered nightly;
Daily round its flowers the wild bees flew.

Sorrow passed, and plucked the golden blossom;
Guilt stripped off the foliage in its pride;
But, within its parent's kindly bosom,
Flowed for ever Life's restoring tide.

Little mourned I for the parted gladness,
For the vacant nest and silent song –
Hope was there, and laughed me out of sadness;
Whispering, 'Winter will not linger long!'

And, behold! with tenfold increase blessing,
Spring adorned the beauty-burdened spray;
Wind and rain and fervent heat, caressing,
Lavished glory on that second May!

High it rose – no winged grief could sweep it;
Sin was scared to distance with its shine;
Love, and its own life, had power to keep it
From all wrong – from every blight but thine!

Cruel Death! The young leaves droop and languish;
Evening's gentle air may still restore –
No! the morning sunshine mocks my anguish –
Time, for me, must never blossom more!

Strike it down, that other boughs may flourish
Where that perished sapling used to be;
Thus, at least, its mouldering corpse will nourish
That from which it sprung – Eternity.

17. Stanzas to —

Well, some may hate, and some may scorn,
And some may quite forget thy name;
But my sad heart must ever mourn
Thy ruined hopes, thy blighted fame!
'Twas thus I thought, an hour ago,
Even weeping o'er that wretch's woe;
One word turned back my gushing tears,
And lit my altered eye with sneers.
Then 'Bless the friendly dust,' I said,
'That hides thy unlamented head!
Vain as thou wert, and weak as vain,
The slave of Falsehood, Pride, and Pain, –
My heart has nought akin to thine;
Thy soul is powerless over mine.'

But these were thoughts that vanished too;
Unwise, unholy, and untrue:
Do I despise the timid deer,
Because his limbs are fleet with fear?
Or, would I mock the wolf's death-howl,
Because his form is gaunt and foul?
Or, hear with joy the leveret's cry,
Because it cannot bravely die?
No! Then above his memory
Let Pity's heart as tender be;
Say, 'Earth, lie lightly on that breast
And, kind Heaven, grant that spirit rest!'

18. Honour's Martyr

The moon is full this winter night;
    The stars are clear, though few;
And every window glistens bright,
    With leaves of frozen dew.

The sweet moon through your lattice gleams
    And lights your room like day;
And there you pass, in happy dreams,
    The peaceful hours away!

While I, with effort hardly quelling
    The anguish in my breast,
Wander about the silent dwelling,
    And cannot think of rest.

The old clock in the gloomy hall
    Ticks on, from hour to hour;
And every time its measured call
    Seems lingering slow and slower:

And oh, how slow that keen-eyed star
    Has tracked the chilly grey!
What, watching yet! how very far
    The morning lies away!

Without your chamber door I stand;
    Love, are you slumbering still?
My cold heart, underneath my hand,
    Has almost ceased to thrill.

Bleak, bleak the east wind sobs and sighs,
    And drowns the turret bell,
Whose sad note, undistinguished, dies
    Unheard, like my farewell!

Tomorrow, Scorn will blight my name,
    And Hate will trample me,
Will load me with a coward's shame –
    A traitor's perjury.

False friends will launch their covert sneers;
    True friends will wish me dead;
And I shall cause the bitterest tears
    That you have ever shed.

The dark deeds of my outlawed race
    Will then like virtues shine;
And men will pardon their disgrace,
    Beside the guilt of mine.

For, who forgives the accursed crime
    Of dastard treachery?
Rebellion, in its chosen time,
    May Freedom's champion be;

Revenge may stain a righteous sword,
    It may be just to slay;
But, traitor, traitor, – from *that* word
    All true breasts shrink away!

Oh, I would give my heart to death,
    To keep my honour fair;
Yet, I'll not give my inward faith
    My honour's *name* to spare!

Not even to keep your priceless love,
    Dare I, Beloved, deceive;
This treason should the future prove,
    Then, only then, believe!

I know the path I ought to go;
    I follow fearlessly,
Inquiring not what deeper woe
    Stern duty stores for me.

So foes pursue, and cold allies
    Mistrust me, every one:
Let me be false in others' eyes,
    If faithful in my own.

19. Stanzas

I'll not weep that thou art going to leave me,
    There's nothing lovely here;
And doubly will the dark world grieve me,
    While thy heart suffers there.

I'll not weep, because the summer's glory
    Must always end in gloom;
And, follow out the happiest story –
    It closes with a tomb!

And I am weary of the anguish
    Increasing winters bear;
Weary to watch the spirit languish
    Through years of dead despair.

So, if a tear, when thou art dying,
    Should haply fall from me,
It is but that my soul is sighing,
    To go and rest with thee.

20. My Comforter

Well hast thou spoken, and yet, not taught
    A feeling strange or new;
Thou hast but roused a latent thought,
A cloud-closed beam of sunshine, brought
    To gleam in open view.

Deep down, concealed within my soul,
    That light lies hid from men;
Yet, glows unquenched – though shadows roll,
Its gentle ray cannot control,
    About the sullen den.

Was I not vexed, in these gloomy ways
    To walk alone so long?
Around me, wretches uttering praise,
Or howling o'er their hopeless days,
    And each with Frenzy's tongue; –

A brotherhood of misery,
    Their smiles as sad as sighs;
Whose madness daily maddened me,
Distorting into agony
    The bliss before my eyes!

So stood I, in Heaven's glorious sun,
    And in the glare of Hell;
My spirit drank a mingled tone,
Of seraph's song, and demon's moan;
What my soul bore, my soul alone
    Within itself may tell!

Like a soft air, above a sea,
    Tossed by the tempest's stir;
A thaw-wind, melting quietly
The snow-drift, on some wintry lea;
No: what sweet thing resembles thee,
    My thoughtful Comforter?

And yet a little longer speak,
    Calm this resentful mood;
And while the savage heart grows meek,
For other token do not seek,
But let the tear upon my cheek
    Evince my gratitude!

21. The Old Stoic

Riches I hold in light esteem;
    And Love I laugh to scorn;
And lust of fame was but a dream
    That vanished with the morn:

And if I pray, the only prayer
    That moves my lips for me
Is, 'Leave the heart that now I bear,
    And give me liberty!'

Yes, as my swift days near their goal,
    'Tis all that I implore;
In life and death, a chainless soul,
    With courage to endure.

22.

Woods you need not frown on me
Spectral trees that so dolefully
Shake your heads in the dreary sky
You need not mock so bitterly

23.

The blue bell is the sweetest flower
That waves in summer air
Its blossoms have the mightiest power
To soothe my spirit's care

There is a spell in purple heath
Too wildly, sadly drear
The violet has a fragrant breath
But fragrance will not cheer

The trees are bare, the sun is cold
And seldom, seldom seen –
The heavens have lost their zone of gold
The earth its robe of green

And ice upon the glancing stream
Has cast its sombre shade
And distant hills and valleys seem
In frozen mist arrayed –

The blue bell cannot charm me now
The heath has lost its bloom
The violets in the glen below
They yield no sweet perfume

But though I mourn the heather-bell
'Tis better far, away
I know how fast my tears would swell
To see it smile today

And that wood flower that hides so shy
Beneath the mossy stone
Its balmy scent and dewy eye
'Tis not for them I moan

It is the slight and stately stem
The blossom's silvery blue
The buds hid like a sapphire gem
In sheaths of emerald hue

'Tis these that breathe upon my heart
A calm and softening spell
That if it makes the tear-drop start
Has power to soothe as well

For these I weep, so long divided
Through winter's dreary day
In longing weep – but most when guided
On withered banks to stray

If chilly then the light should fall
Adown the dreary sky
And gild the dank and darkened wall
With transient brilliancy

How do I yearn, how do I pine
For the time of flowers to come
And turn me from that fading shine
To mourn the fields of home –

24. The Night-Wind

In summer's mellow midnight
A cloudless moon shone through
Our open parlour window
And rosetrees wet with dew

I sat in silent musing –
The soft wind waved my hair
It told me Heaven was glorious
And sleeping Earth was fair –

I needed not its breathing
To bring such thoughts to me
But still it whispered lowly
'How dark the woods will be! –

'The thick leaves in my murmur
Are rustling like a dream,
And all their myriad voices
Instinct with spirit seem'

I said, 'Go gentle singer,
Thy wooing voice is kind
But do not think its music
Has power to reach my mind –

'Play with the scented flower,
The young tree's supple bough –
And leave my human feelings
In their own course to flow'

The Wanderer would not leave me
Its kiss grew warmer still –
'O come,' it sighed so sweetly
'I'll win thee 'gainst thy will –

'Have we not been from childhood friends?
Have I not loved thee long?
As long as thou hast loved the night
Whose silence wakes my song?

'And when thy heart is laid at rest
Beneath the church-yard stone
I shall have time enough to mourn
And thou to be alone' –

25.

The night is darkening round me
The wild winds coldly blow
But a tyrant spell has bound me
And I cannot cannot go

The giant trees are bending
Their bare boughs weighed with snow
And the storm is fast descending
And yet I cannot go

Clouds beyond clouds above me
Wastes beyond wastes below
But nothing drear can move me
I will not cannot go

— — — — —

I'll come when thou art saddest
Laid alone in the darkened room
When the mad day's mirth has vanished
And the smile of joy is banished
From evening's chilly gloom

I'll come when the heart's [real] feeling
Has entire unbiased sway
And my influence o'er thee stealing
Grief deepening joy congealing
Shall bear thy soul away

Listen 'tis just the hour
The awful time for thee
Dost thou not feel upon thy soul
A flood of strange sensations roll
Forerunners of a sterner power
Heralds of me

——————

I would have touched the heavenly key
That spoke alike of bliss and thee
I would have woke the entrancing song
But its words died upon my tongue
And then I knew that hallowed strain
Could never speak of joy again
And then I felt

26.

Shall Earth no more inspire thee,
Thou lonely dreamer now?
Since passion may not fire thee
Shall Nature cease to bow?

Thy mind is ever moving
In regions dark to thee;
Recall its useless roving –
Come back and dwell with me –

I know my mountain breezes
Enchant and soothe thee still –
I know my sunshine pleases
Despite thy wayward will –

When day with evening blending
Sinks from the summer sky,
I've seen thy spirit bending
In fond idolatry –

I've watched thee every hour –
I know my mighty sway –
I know my magic power
To drive thy griefs away –

Few hearts to mortals given
On earth so wildly pine
Yet none would ask a Heaven
More like this Earth than thine –

Then let my winds caress thee –
Thy comrade let me be –
Since nought beside can bless thee
Return and dwell with me –

27.

No coward soul is mine
No trembler in the world's storm-troubled sphere
I see Heaven's glories shine
And Faith shines equal arming me from Fear

O God within my breast
Almighty ever-present Deity
Life, that in me hast rest
As I Undying Life, have power in thee

Vain are the thousand creeds
That move men's hearts, unutterably vain,
Worthless as withered weeds
Or idlest froth amid the boundless main

To waken doubt in one
Holding so fast by thy infinity
So surely anchored on
The steadfast rock of Immortality

With wide-embracing love
Thy spirit animates eternal years
Pervades and broods above,
Changes, sustains, dissolves, creates and rears

Though Earth and moon were gone
And suns and universes ceased to be
And thou wert left alone
Every Existence would exist in thee

There is not room for Death
Nor atom that his might could render void
Since thou art Being and Breath
And what thou art may never be destroyed

28.

All hushed and still within the house
Without – all wind and driving rain
But something whispers to my mind
Through rain and [through the] wailing wind
                    – Never again
Never again? Why not again?
Memory has power as real as thine

29.

Often rebuked, yet always back returning
    To those first feelings that were born with me,
And leaving busy chase of wealth and learning
    For idle dreams of things which cannot be:

Today, I will seek not the shadowy region;
    Its unsustaining vastness waxes drear;
And visions rising, legion after legion,
    Bring the unreal world too strangely near.

I'll walk, but not in old heroic traces,
    And not in paths of high morality,
And not among the half-distinguished faces,
    The clouded forms of long-past history.

I'll walk where my own nature would be leading:
    It vexes me to choose another guide:
Where the grey flocks in ferny glens are feeding;
    Where the wild wind blows on the mountain side.

What have those lonely mountains worth revealing?
    More glory and more grief than I can tell:
The earth that wakes *one* human heart to feeling
    Can centre both the worlds of Heaven and Hell.

Why ask to know what date what clime
There dwelt our own humanity
Power-worshippers from earliest time
Foot-kissers of triumphant crime
Crushers of helpless misery
Crushing down Justice honouring Wrong
If that be feeble this be strong

Shedders of blood shedders of tears
Self-cursers avid of distress
Yet Mocking heaven with senseless prayers
For mercy on the merciless

It was the autumn of the year
When grain grows yellow in the ear
Day after day from noon to noon,
That August's sun blazed bright as June

But we with unregarding eyes
Saw panting earth and glowing skies
No hand the reaper's sickle held
Nor bound the ripe sheaves in the field

Our corn was garnered months before,
Threshed out and kneaded-up with gore
Ground when the ears were milky sweet
With furious toil of hoofs and feet
I doubly cursed on foreign sod
Fought neither for my home nor God